GOOGLE DRIVE FOR BUSINESS

The ultimate guide for beginners to enhance workflow

CONTENTS

Introduction

Chapter 1: Google Drive

Overview of Google Drive

How to create a Google account

Chapter 2: Setting Up Your Google Drive

Accessing Google Drive

Understanding the basic folders and options

Chapter 3: Uploading and Organizing Files

Uploading files and folders

Organizing content effectively

Chapter 4: Collaboration and Sharing

Sharing files and folders with team members

Setting access permissions

Chapter 5: Google Drive for Team

Collaboration

Creating and managing teams

Collaborative document editing

Chapter 6: Integrating Google Drive with Other Tools

Integrating Google Drive with Gmail

Third-party integrations and add-ons

Chapter 7: Security and Privacy

Google Drive security features

Chapter 8: Automating Workflows with Google Drive

Streamlining business processes

Chapter 9: Mobile Access and Offline Mode

Accessing Google Drive on mobile devices

Working offline with Google Drive

Syncing files for offline access

INTRODUCTION

Here's the place to be if you've ever pondered how to streamline file management, increase teamwork, and improve productivity in your company. We're going to take a journey through the pages that follow to help you understand Google Drive's capabilities and realize all of its possibilities for your work-related needs.

In a world where seamless collaboration and efficient file sharing are the keys to success, Google Drive stands tall as a versatile and user-friendly tool that can revolutionize the way you and your team work together. Whether you're a seasoned entrepreneur, a small business owner, or just someone eager to enhance your digital skills, this book is designed to guide you through the ins and outs of Google Drive, making it your ultimate ally in the business world.

But hey, we get it – technology can be overwhelming. That's why we've crafted this guide with simplicity in mind. No jargon, no tech-speak – just plain, straightforward advice to help you harness the power of Google Drive without breaking a sweat.

Why You Need to Read This Book

- Learn how Google Drive can streamline your file management, saving you time and energy in your day-to-day operations.

- Discover the secrets of effective collaboration, enabling your team to work seamlessly on projects, no matter where they are.
- Uncover tips and tricks to make your work more efficient, allowing you to focus on what matters most – growing your business.
- Understand the security features of Google Drive, ensuring your data is protected in the digital landscape.
- Stay ahead of the curve by mastering a tool that continues to evolve. This knowledge will keep you adaptable in the ever-changing world of technology.

So, lets dive into the exciting realm of Google Drive. By the end of this journey, you'll not only be a Google Drive pro, but you'll also be equipped to take your business collaboration to new heights.

CHAPTER 1
Google Drive

Overview of Google Drive

Imagine having a magical space in the digital realm where all your important files, documents, and cat memes are neatly organized and accessible from anywhere. Well, that's basically Google Drive – your virtual superhero for all things file-related.

Google Drive is like the Swiss Army knife of the internet, but for your files. It's a cloud-based storage service by Google that lets you store, access, and share your files securely. It's not just a place to dump stuff; it's a dynamic platform that can seriously up your collaboration game.

Your Digital File Cabinet:
Envision Google Drive as your digital filing cupboard. You have files and folders that are well-organized and prepared for use, saving you from having to search through mountains of paper. Drive is the place to store everything, including spreadsheets you're

secretly proud of, work documents, and pictures.

Anytime, Anywhere Access:
The coolest part? It's not chained to your computer. With Google Drive, your stuff is on the cloud, meaning you can access it from your laptop, phone, tablet, or even your neighbour's computer if you're feeling adventurous. As long as you have an internet connection, your files are at your fingertips.

Collaboration Nirvana:

Now, here's where it gets exciting. Google Drive isn't just a solitary experience. It's like a digital playground for teamwork. You can share files with teammates, work on them together in real-time, and leave comments like virtual sticky notes. Collaboration has never been this easy – or this fun.

No More Attachment Hassles:
Bid farewell to the stress that comes with exchanging files via email. You can give your colleague immediate access to your work by sharing a link to it using Drive. Additionally, you

are in charge of who can see or modify your work, so you may keep things as secret or public as you like.

Docs, Sheets, Slides:
Google Drive comes with a family of apps – Google Docs, Sheets, Slides, and more. These aren't your average applications; they're like the Avengers of productivity. They live in the cloud, allowing seamless collaboration, and changes are saved automatically. No more frantic searching for the "Save" button.
So, in a nutshell, Google Drive is your digital command centre. It's

where your files live happily, where collaboration becomes a breeze, and where you can kiss goodbye to the hassle of version control. It's not just storage; it's a game-changer for how you work, share, and create in the digital age.

How to create a Google account

Visit the Sign-Up Page: First things first, open your web browser and go to the Google account creation page. You can do this by typing "create Google account" into the search bar.

Google's got your back; it's usually the first result.

Fill in the Blanks: You'll see a form requesting some information. Just the essentials, like your first and last names—nothing too personal. Next, select a username. Since this will be your email address, choose an email address that you are comfortable sharing with others.

Create a password: This is like the secret handshake to your account, so make it strong. Google will give you some tips to ensure it's robust enough. And don't forget – keep it safe like grandma's secret cookie recipe.

Phone Number & Recovery Email: Adding a phone number and a recovery email is like having a spare key to your digital home. If you ever get locked out, Google can send you a magic link to get back in. It's your personal escape route.

Prove You're Not a Robot: Google wants to make sure you're not a sneaky robot trying to sneak in. They might ask you to prove you're human by solving a puzzle or typing in some squiggly letters. It's their way of keeping the internet a robot-free zone.

Agree to the Terms: Nobody likes reading the fine print, but it's essential. Scroll through the terms of service and privacy policy, and if you're cool with it (which you probably are), click that "I agree" button. You're almost there!

Welcome to Your Google Home: You're officially a Google account owner. Welcome to the club! Now, you can explore Google Drive, Gmail, and all the other cool features Google has in store for you.

CHAPTER 2

Setting Up Your Google Drive

Accessing Google Drive

- Open Your Web Browser: Grab your computer, open your favourite web browser (Chrome, Firefox, Safari, you name it).
- Go to Google: Type "Google" into the search bar or just go straight to www.google.com.
- Sign In to Your Google Account: There's a "Sign In"

button in the upper right corner. You'll be asked to enter your Google account email address and password after clicking that. Don't worry if you don't have an account! To create an account, click "Create account" and proceed as directed.

- The Grid Icon: Once you're signed in, look for a little grid of squares (some call it the waffle) in the top right corner. Click on it.
- Find the Drive Icon: Among the icons that pop up, you're

looking for one that looks like a triangle with three circles – that's your Google Drive! Click on it.

- Welcome to Google Drive: You're now in your Google Drive. This is your digital space where you can store files, collaborate with others, and generally be a productivity ninja.

Understanding the basic options

- My Drive: This is like the main living room. Everything you upload or create lands here. It's your personal space. Create folders, toss in files – it's your digital playground.

- Shared with Me: Imagine this as your "Received Invitations" box. Any files or folders someone shared with you will be hanging out here. It's your VIP pass to collaboration.
- Recent: This is your virtual time machine. It shows the files you've been working on recently, saving you the hassle of digging through folders to find that elusive document.

- Starred: Think of this like your gold-starred homework from the teacher. If there are files or folders you want quick access to, just star them, and they'll hang out here for easy retrieval.
- Trash: Oops, did you accidentally delete something? No worries. Your digital trash can is here to catch it. Anything you delete stays here until you decide to empty the trash or recover your lost treasure.

CHAPTER 3

Uploading and Organizing Files

Uploading files and folders

- Find the "+ New" Button: Look for the "+ New" button on the left side as soon as you are in you google drive. It's your magic wand for creating and uploading.
- Uploading Files: Click on "+ New" and then select "File upload." A window will pop up. Now, find the file on your

computer that you want in your Drive, click on it, and hit "Open." Boom, you just uploaded a file!

- Creating a Folder: Want to keep things organized? Click "+ New" again, but this time choose "Folder." Give your folder a snazzy name. Now, you've got a cozy place to stash your files.

- Uploading Folders: Google Drive is cool – it can handle folders too! Just click "+ New," then "Folder upload." Find the folder on your computer, click "Select Folder," and watch it zip into your Drive.

- Drag and Drop Magic: Open your file explorer (Windows) or Finder (Mac), find your files or folders, click and hold, drag them over to your Google Drive, and drop them. It's like magic – they'll upload right then and there.

- Organize as You Go: When you upload, Google Drive might ask you where you want things. Pick a folder or just let it land in "My Drive." You can always organize later.

- Check Your Recent: Once you've uploaded, click on "Recent" in the left menu. Your latest uploads will be right there, ready for action.

Organizing content effectively

- Move Files Around: Click on a file to select it. See those icons at the top? Click the folder icon, and you can move it wherever you want. Think of it as file teleportation.

- Use Colours to Jazz Things Up: Want to add a splash of colour to your folders? Right-click on a folder, go to "Change color," and pick your favorite hue. It's like decorating your digital space.
- Star Important Stuff: Got files or folders you need quick access to? Click on them, hit the star icon, and they'll hang out in the "Starred" section for easy retrieval.
- Sort Your View: Click on "My Drive" on the left. See those sort options up top? You can

arrange your files and folders by name, date modified, or last opened. It's like having your own digital secretary.

- "Shared with Me": Working together with others? "Shared with Me" may be hopping right now. Remember to put these files into folders as well.

- Clear Out the Trash: Deleted something? It's probably in the trash. Click on "Trash" on the left, select the things you want to permanently delete or recover, and click the buttons up top.

- Search Like a Pro: If you are feeling lost, Use the search bar. It's like having a personal detective. Type a keyword, and Google Drive will find your file faster than you can say "organization ninja."
- Embrace Subfolders: Do you want to step up the organizing game? Make folders inside of folders. Like drawers inside your electronic filing cabinet.

CHAPTER 4

Collaboration and Sharing

Sharing files and folders with team members

- Find the File or Folder You Want to Share: Scroll through "My Drive" or "Shared with Me" to find the file or folder you're itching to share. Click on it to select it.

- Click the "Share" Button: See that little icon that looks like a person with a plus sign? Yep, that's your "Share" button. Click on it.

- Choose Who to Share With: A box will pop up. Enter the email addresses of the teammates you want to share with. If they're in your contacts, Google Drive might suggest them as you type.
- Set Permissions: You should notice a dropdown menu with the word "Viewer" underneath the email field. Simply click it to view your alternatives. It is up to you to decide if your teammates can only view, comment, or Edit the document.

- Add a Message: Want to add a personal touch? Below the email box, you can write a little message to your team. It's like a digital sticky note.
- Click "Send": Once you've set everything up, hit the "Send" button. Your team will get an email with a link to the file or folder.
- Sharing Folders: Sharing folders is just as easy. Click on the folder, hit the "Share" button, and follow the same steps. Everyone with access to the folder gets access to

everything inside it. It's like sharing a whole desk instead of just one document.

- Check Who Has Access: Want to see who can view, comment, or edit your file or folder? Click on "Share" again, and you'll see the list of people with access. If you need to change permissions, click on the dropdown next to their name.
- Stop Sharing: Changed your mind? Click "Share" again, find the person you want to

remove, and click the "X" next to their name. Poof, they're out.

Setting access permissions

- Set Permissions: Right below the email box, you'll spot a dropdown menu that says "Viewer." Click on it, and you've got options:
- **Viewer:** They can look but not touch.
- **Commenter:** They can leave notes and comments, like digital post-its.

- **Editor:** They're the VIPs – they can edit, add, and delete stuff.

- Advanced Settings (Optional): Need to fine-tune permissions? Click on "Advanced" in the bottom right. Here, you can control link sharing, disable downloading, and more. It's like having a secret menu.

- Change Permissions Later: Say you want to change someone's status. Click "Share" again, find their email, and click on the dropdown next to their name. Adjust the permissions – easy peasy.

CHAPTER 5
Google Drive for Team Collaboration

Creating and managing teams

- Create a Team Folder: Want a cozy space just for your team? Create a special folder for your team files. Click "+ New" on the left, choose "Folder," and name it something catchy.
- Drop Files into the Team Folder: If you made a team folder, drag and drop your files

into it. It's like having your team's stuff all in one place.

- Set Team Folder Access: Click on the team folder, hit the "Share" button again, and set the permissions just like you did for individual files.
- Add or Remove Team Members: Click on "Share" once more to see your current team. To add someone, type in their email and set their permissions. To remove someone, click on the "X" next to their name.

- Team Communication: Want to keep the team in the loop? Create a Google Chat room or use other communication tools to discuss files, share updates, and collaborate seamlessly.
- Team Notifications: Let your team know when things change. When you share or un share files, there's an option to send notifications. Keep everyone in the loop!
- Check the Team Activity: Curious about what your team has been up to? In Google Drive, click on "Recent" to see

the most recent activity across all files.

Collaborative document editing

- Real-Time Collaboration Magic: When your team opens the document, you'll see each other's cursors. It's like a virtual room where everyone has their own colour. Start typing, and watch the magic happen in real-time.
- Comment Like a Pro: Want to leave notes or suggestions without changing the text? Highlight a word, right-click,

and choose "Comment." It's like whispering a suggestion without interrupting the main conversation.

- Check Revision History: If things get wild and you need to time-travel, click on "File" at the top, then "Version history," and finally, "See version history." You can review changes and even revert to an earlier version if needed.

CHAPTER 6

Integrating Google Drive with Other Tools

Integrating Google Drive with Gmail

- Open Gmail: First things first, let's hop into your Gmail account. If you're not there yet, open your web browser, go to www.gmail.com, and sign in.

- Compose a New Email: Click on the red "+ Compose" button to start a new email. You know, the virtual equivalent of grabbing a fresh sheet of paper.

- Find the Google Drive Icon: Look for the Google Drive icon at the bottom of the new email window. It's a little triangle with a paperclip. Click on it.
- Choose Your Files: A window will pop up showing your Google Drive files. You can pick the files you want to share by clicking on them. It's like picking toppings for your digital pizza.
- Insert the Files: Once you've selected your files, click the "Insert" button. Your chosen

files are now attached to your email, ready to be sent.

- Adjust Sharing Settings (Optional): Before sending, you can adjust the sharing settings. Click on the "Drive" icon again, select the file, and click on the little pencil icon to manage who can access the file. It's like setting the backstage pass level.

- Add Recipients and Message: Now, add the email addresses of the recipients, and type in your message if you want. It's like adding a personal note to your digital delivery.

- Click "Send": Once everything looks good, hit the "Send" button. Your email, complete with the attached Google Drive files, is on its way.
- Drive Link Instead of Attachment: If your file is too large or you want to keep things neat, you can choose to send a Drive link instead of attaching the actual file. Click on the Drive icon, hover over the file, and click on the chain link icon.

Third-party integrations and add-ons

- Find Your Document: Locate the document where you want to unleash the magic. Click on it to open.
- Click "Add-ons" in the Top Menu: At the top of the document, you'll see a menu. Click on "Add-ons." It's like opening a secret compartment in your toolbox.
- Choose "Get Add-ons": A dropdown menu will appear.

Click on "Get add-ons." It's like entering the app store for your Google Drive.

- Browse the Add-ons Store: You'll be taken to the Google Workspace Marketplace. Here, you can explore a variety of add-ons for different purposes – from productivity to creativity.
- Find an Add-on You Like: Browse the categories or use the search bar to find an add-on that suits your needs. Click on it to learn more.

- Click "Install": Found the perfect add-on? Click "Install." It's like adding a new gadget to your toolbox.
- Grant Permissions: The add-on might need some permissions to function. Review them and click "Allow" if you're comfortable. It's like giving your new tool the keys to the toolbox.
- Access the Add-on: Once installed, the add-on will appear in the "Add-ons" menu. You can usually access it from

there. It's like having a new button on your toolbelt.

- Explore Features: Click on the add-on, explore its features, and see how it enhances your Google Drive experience. It's like discovering a new function on your favourite gadget.

CHAPTER 7
Security and Privacy

Google Drive security features

- Two-Factor Authentication (2FA): Think of this as having not one but two secret handshakes. With 2FA, even if someone gets hold of your password, they still need that second piece – usually a code sent to your phone. Activate it in your Google Account settings for an extra layer of protection.

- Encryption on Transit and at Rest: Your data is like a secret message, and Google Drive ensures it stays safe during delivery and when it's just chilling. It's encrypted when moving between your device and Google servers (in transit) and when stored on Google servers (at rest).
- Suspicious Activity Alerts: Google Drive is like your vigilant security guard. If it detects unusual sign-in activities or access patterns, it'll shoot you an alert. It's like

having a superhero sense for potential threats.

- Secure File Sharing: When you share files or folders, you're in control. You can decide who can view, comment, or edit. You can also generate shareable links with specific permissions. It's like giving out special keys that only work for certain doors.

- Version History: Imagine having a time machine for your documents. Google Drive's version history lets you review changes made to your files. If something fishy happens, you can revert to a previous, safer version. It's like undo for your entire document.

- Advanced Protection Program (APP): If you're a high-risk user – maybe a political activist or a journalist working on sensitive topics – Google offers the Advanced Protection Program. It's like having a personal bodyguard for your Google Account.

- Data Loss Prevention (DLP): Google Drive is your watchful eye for sensitive information.

DLP lets you set policies to prevent sharing of confidential stuff. It's like having a bouncer at the door who checks IDs before letting anyone in.

- Device Management: Ever left your phone at the coffee shop? With Google Drive's device management, you can remotely sign out of your account on that lost device. It's like having a self-destruct button for your Google Drive access.
- Safe Browsing: Google Drive checks the URLs in your files to make sure they're not

leading you into a trap. It's like having a trustworthy guide who ensures you don't wander into sketchy neighborhoods on the internet.

- Activity Dashboard: This is your personal detective board. The activity dashboard shows you who's been peeking into your files and when. It's like having a logbook for your documents.

Chapter 8
Automating Workflows with Google Drive

Streamlining business processes

- Centralize Your Hub: Start by creating a central folder in Google Drive for all your business-related documents. It's like having a headquarters where everyone knows to go for the good stuff.
- Folder Organization: Within that central hub, create folders for different departments, projects, or processes. Think of

them like neatly labeled drawers – Finance, Marketing, Project A, Project B, you get the idea.

- Naming Conventions: Be the maestro of consistency. Establish clear naming conventions for files and folders. It's like having a secret code that everyone in your business understands. For example, "ProjectX_Report_Q1_2024."
- Template Wonderland: Create templates for recurring documents. If you have

standard forms, proposals, or reports, save them as templates. It's like having the blueprint ready for every new project or task.

- Share and Collaborate: Use Google Drive's sharing features wisely. Collaborate on documents in real-time. It's like having a virtual office where everyone contributes to the masterpiece.
- Set Permissions Smartly: Control who can view, comment, or edit files. It's like having different levels of

security clearance. Your finance team might have the keys to the treasure chest, but not everyone needs that level of access.

- Automate with Google Forms: Streamline data collection with Google Forms. Create forms for surveys, feedback, or internal requests. The data goes straight to a Google Sheet, making analysis a breeze. It's like having a digital suggestion box.

- Integrate with Google Calendar: Schedule meetings,

deadlines, and project milestones using Google Calendar. Link relevant documents from Google Drive directly in your calendar events. It's like having your schedule and resources in one place.

- Use Google Workspace Apps: Leverage Google Docs, Sheets, and Slides for collaborative work. Whether it's drafting documents, analyzing data, or creating presentations, these apps are your trusty sidekicks.

- Explore Google Chat and Meet: Communicate seamlessly with your team using Google Chat. Initiate video meetings with Google Meet directly from Google Drive. It's like having a virtual water cooler for quick chats and team huddles.
- Version Control: Keep track of changes with version history. It's like having a time machine – if something goes wrong, you can always go back to a previous version.

- Use App Integrations: Integrate other apps your business uses with Google Drive. Whether it's project management tools, CRM systems, or communication platforms, streamline your workflow by connecting the dots.
- Regular Audits: Conduct periodic reviews of your folder structure and file organization. It's like cleaning out the clutter in your office – a tidy space leads to a tidy mind.
- Train Your Team: Educate your team on best practices for

using Google Drive. It's like giving everyone the same playbook, ensuring smooth collaboration.

CHAPTER 9
Mobile Access and Offline Mode

Accessing Google Drive on mobile devices

For Android Devices:

- Download Google Drive App: If you haven't already, head to the Google Play Store, search for "Google Drive," and hit that install button. It's like getting the key to your virtual workspace.

- Sign In: If you're not signed in, enter your Google account credentials. It's like swiping your badge to access your workspace.
- Navigate Your Drive: Inside the app, you'll see your files and folders. Swipe and tap to navigate – it's like flipping through documents on your desk.
- Upload Files: Want to add a new file from your phone? Tap the "+" button, and you can upload photos, videos, or any other file from your device. It's

like placing a new document on your desk.

- Edit Docs on the Go: Need to make quick edits to a Google Doc? Tap on the document, and you can make changes right from your phone. It's like having a miniature editor in your pocket.
- Share and Collaborate: Tap and hold on a file to select it, then tap the share icon. You can send files to others, just like passing notes in class. It's like collaborating, but with a digital twist.

For iOS Devices (iPhone/iPad):

- Download Google Drive App: Head to the App Store, search for "Google Drive," and download the app. It's like adding a new app to your home screen.

- Open the App: Once installed, open the Google Drive app. Sign in with your Google account – it's like getting your mobile workspace ready.

- Explore Your Drive: Inside the app, you'll see your files. Swipe and tap to explore – it's like flipping through your digital folders.

- Upload Files: Need to add something new? Tap the "+" button, and you can upload files from your device. It's like placing new items on your digital desk.
- Edit Docs Anywhere: If you have Google Docs, Sheets, or Slides, you can edit them on the go. Open a document, and it's like having a tiny office suite in your pocket.
- Share the Goodies: Tap and hold on a file, then tap the

share icon. You can share files with others or collaborate in real-time. It's like having a mobile meeting room.

Syncing files for offline access

- Install Backup and Sync: Make sure Google Backup and Sync is installed on your computer before anything else. Download and install it if you don't already have it. It's similar to setting up a private file courier.
- Open Google Drive Folder: Navigate to your Google Drive

folder on your computer. It's like opening the door to your digital workspace.

- Right-Click on Files/Folders: Right-click on the file or folder you want to access offline. A menu will pop up – choose "Available offline." It's like telling your computer, "I need these files with me at all times."
- Check Sync Status: You'll see a tiny syncing icon (two arrows forming a circle) next to the files or folders. It's like a little superhero cape, indicating they

are ready to be your offline work buddies.

- Access Offline Files: Once synced, you can access these files even when your computer is not connected to the internet. It's like having your favorite documents in your backpack wherever you go.

- Automatic Updates: Any changes you make to these files offline will automatically sync with Google Drive when you're back online. It's like having your personal assistant ensuring everything stays up to date.

Working offline with Google Drive

- Install Backup and Sync: First things first, make sure you have Google's Backup and Sync installed on your computer. It's like the secret sauce that allows you to sync your Google Drive with your computer.

- Enable Offline Mode: Open Google Drive on your computer and right-click on the file or folder you want to access offline. Select "Available offline." It's like making a playlist of your favorite work files.

- Access Files in Google Drive Folder: Once you've marked files for offline access, you can find them in your Google Drive folder on your computer. It's like having a portable office right on your device.
- Work on Files: Open the files as you normally would. Edit your documents, spreadsheets, or presentations – it's like you never left the office.

- Changes Sync When Online: When you're back online, any changes you made offline will automatically sync with Google Drive. It's like your virtual assistant making sure everything is up to date.

Made in the USA
Monee, IL
10 August 2024